What Can Jump?

Patricia Whitehouse

Heinemann Library
Chicago, Illinois

Designed by Sue Emerson, Heinemann Library; Page layout by Que-Net Media™
Printed and bound in the U.S.A. by Lake Book Manufacturing
Photo research by Bill Broyles

08 07 06 05 04
10 9 8 7 6 5 4 3 2 1

Library of Congress Cataloging-in-Publication Data
Whitehouse, Patricia, 1958-
    What can jump? / Patricia Whitehouse.
        v. cm. – (What can?)
Includes index.
Contents: What is jumping? – How do living things jump? – Can small animals jump? – Can big animals jump? – Can animals with webbed feet jump? – Can bugs jump? – Can beans jump? – Can machines jump? – Can people jump?
    ISBN 1-4034-4366-1 (HC), 1-4034-4373-4 (Pbk.)
    1. Jumping–Juvenile literature. 2. Animal jumping–Juvenile literature. [1. Jumping. 2. Animal jumping.] I. Title.
    QP310.J86W48 2003
    573.7'91–dc21

2003001016

Acknowledgments
The author and publishers are grateful to the following for permission to reproduce copyright material:
pp. 4, 5, 10 Stephen J. Krasemann/DRK Photo; p. 6 Erwin Nielsen/Visuals Unlimited; p. 7 S. Dalton/NHPA; p. 8 Satoshi Kuribayashi/OSF/Dark Photo; p. 9 D. Northcott/DRK Photo; p. 11 Ahupa Manoj Shah/DRK Photo; p. 12 Joe McDonald/Visuals Unlimited; p. 13 S. Maslowski/Visuals Unlimited; p. 14 Elliott Bignell/Naturepl.com; p. 15 Paulo De Oliveira/Oxford Scientific Films; p. 16 D. Cavagnaro/DRK Photo; p. 17 Wayne P. Armstrong; p. 18 Robert Lifson/Heinemann Library; p. 19 Randy Montoya/Sandia National Laboratories; p. 20 Jeff Greenberg/Visuals Unlimited; p. 21 Masha Nordry/Bruce Coleman Inc.; p. 22 (row 1, L-R)S. Maslowski/Visuals Unlimited, Wayne P. Armstrong, Satoshi Kuribayashi/OSF/Dark Photo; (row 2, L-R) Elliott Bignell/Naturepl.com, Corbis; p. 23 (row 1, L-R) Ahupa Manoj Shah/DRK Photo, A. Hart-Davis/Photo Researchers, Inc.; (row 2, L-R) D. Northcott/DRK Photo, Robert Lifson/Heinemann Library, S. Maslowski/Visuals Unlimited; (row 3) Randy Montoya/Sandia National Laboratories; p. 24 (row 1, L-R) Corbis, Satoshi Kuribayashi/OSF/Dark Photo, Elliott Bignell/Naturepl.com; (row 2, L-R) S. Maslowski/Visuals Unlimited, Wayne P. Armstrong; back cover (L-R) Stephen J. Krasemann/DRK Photo, Joe McDonald/Visuals Unlimited

Cover photograph by Ahupa Manoj Shah/DRK Photo

Every effort has been made to contact copyright holders of any material reproduced in this book.
Any omissions will be rectified in subsequent printings if notice is given to the publisher.

Special thanks to our advisory panel for their help in the preparation of this book:

Alice Bethke, Library Consultant
Palo Alto, CA

Eileen Day, Preschool Teacher
Chicago, IL

Kathleen Gilbert,
Second Grade Teacher
Round Rock, TX

Sandra Gilbert,
Library Media Specialist
Fiest Elementary School
Houston, TX

Jan Gobeille,
Kindergarten Teacher
Garfield Elementary
Oakland, CA

Angela Leeper,
Educational Consultant
Wake Forest, NC

Some words are shown in bold, **like this.**
You can find them in the picture glossary on page 23.

Contents

What Is Jumping?

Jumping is a way of moving.

Living things that jump start out on the ground.

They hop into the air.

Then they come back down again.

How Do Living Things Jump?

Animals that jump have legs that bend.

Some push themselves up with strong leg **muscles.**

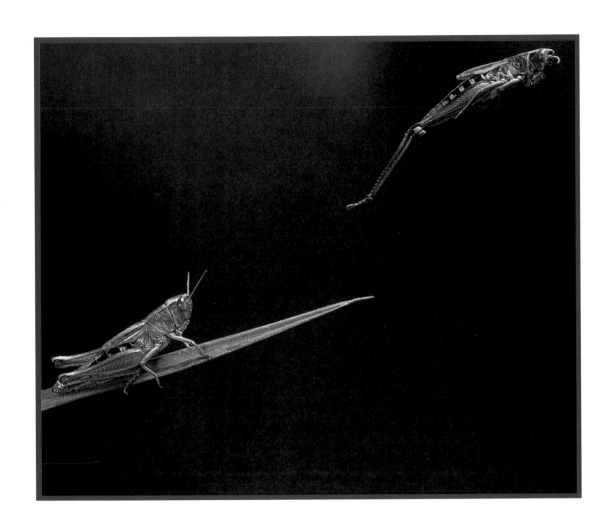

Others have leg parts that are like **springs.**

These parts give the jump an extra push.

Can Small Animals Jump?

Jumping spiders are small.

They can jump across your desk!

Kangaroo rats are small, furry animals.

They can jump across your bedroom in one jump.

Can Big Animals Jump?

Kangaroos are big animals.

They use their strong back legs and feet to jump.

Impalas are big animals.

They can jump up higher than a basketball goal.

Can Animals with Webbed Feet Jump?

Frogs have **webbed feet**.

Frogs use their long back legs to jump.

webbed feet

Ducks have webbed feet, too.

But ducks cannot jump.

Can Bugs Jump?

Crickets are bugs.

They have special leg parts that help them jump.

Fleas are tiny bugs.

They can jump onto dogs
and people.

Can Beans Jump?

Beans grow on plants.

Plants cannot jump.

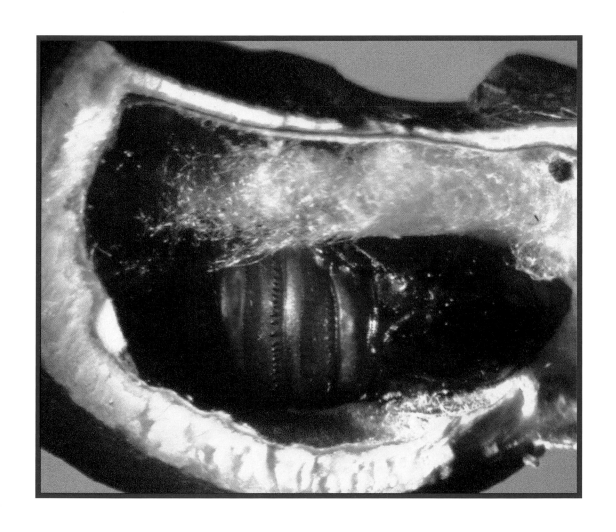

These beans have caterpillars inside.

When the caterpillars move, the bean looks like it is jumping.

Can Machines Jump?

spring

A **pogo stick** is a jumping toy.

A person pushes the **spring** down to make it jump.

robot

Scientists are working on a jumping robot machine.

It may be used to explore other **planets.**

Can People Jump?

People can jump by themselves.

They use their strong leg **muscles** to help them.

People can jump on **trampolines.**

Trampolines give the jump an extra push.

Quiz

Which of these things can jump?

Can you find them in the book?

 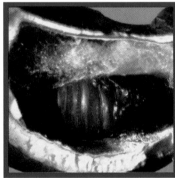 

Picture Glossary

impala
(im-PAH-lah)
page 11

planet
page 19

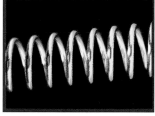

spring
pages 7, 18

kangaroo rat
page 9

pogo stick
page 18

webbed feet
pages 12, 13

muscle
pages 6, 20

robot
page 19

Note to Parents and Teachers

Reading for information is an important part of a child's literacy development. Learning begins with a question about something. Help children think of themselves as investigators and researchers by encouraging their questions about the world around them. Each chapter in this book begins with a question that helps categorize the types of things that jump. Read each question together. Look at the pictures. Can children think of other jumping things in each category? Discuss where you might find the answers. Assist children in using the picture glossary and the index to practice new vocabulary and research skills.

Index

Answers to quiz on page 22

Children, jumping spiders, and crickets can jump.

Ducks cannot jump.
Beans can only jump if they have caterpillars inside them.